A TRAPPER'S GUIDE
TO
AUTISTIC CRITTERS

A Trapper's Guide to Autistic Critters

Soothing the Savage Beastie

Diana P. Catlin

A Trapper's Guide to Autistic Critters
Copyright © 2025 by Diana Catlin
All rights reserved, including the right to reproduce
distribute, or transmit in any form or by any means.

Except as permitted under the U.S. Copyright Act of 1976, no part
of this book may be reproduced, distributed, or transmitted in any
form or by any means, or stored in a database or retrieval system
without the written permission of the authors, except in the case of
brief passages embodied in critical reviews and articles where the
title, author and ISBN accompany such review or article.

For information contact:
dpcatlin@gmail.com

Published by:
Salt & Pepper Legacy Publishing

Cover design and interior design by
Francine Platt, Eden Graphics, Inc.

Paperback ISBN 979-8-89454-033-7

eBook ISBN 979-8-89454-034-4

Audiobook ISBN 979-8-89454-035-1

Library of Congress Control Number: 2024927430

Manufactured in the United States of America
First Edition

To Michael Sorensen—
your idea of blending a trapper's wisdom with
the wild and wonderful world of autism sparked
the inspiration that set this journey in motion.

To my neurodivergent loved ones, who have
taught me patience, resilience, and the beauty
of a mind that sees the world differently.

And to every soul seeking to understand, connect,
and bring calm to the chaos—may this book offer
you both laughter and light along the way.

PREFACE

In *A Trapper's Guide to the Autistic Critter: Soothing the Savage Beastie,* we take a lighthearted yet insightful approach to understanding and addressing the unique challenges of autism. Using humor and vivid analogies from the trapping world, we hope to shed light on practical strategies to help neurodivergent individuals thrive in a world not built with them in mind.

With an emphasis on compassion and empowerment, we explore tools for improving communication, building trust, and creating supportive environments. By embracing humor, we not only normalize challenges, but we also remind each other of the beauty and strength found in diversity.

Whether you're a seasoned "trapper" or just starting to understand the "beastie" in your life, this book will equip you with the skills and mindset to navigate the wilderness of autism with patience, love, and a touch of wit. Prepare to embark on an adventure that's both heartwarming and practical!

This work will contain messages from "**HER**" and "**HIM**". These refer to the author and her spouse. These examples and insights come directly from their life experiences. He is a late diagnosed neurodivergent, autistic man. She is neurotypical.

(HER) As a caretaker, it's too easy to get caught up in the day-to-day details and "must get it done" mind-spaces. To calm, interact with, or simply influence effectively, you must "set the trap" so it appeals to that particular furbaby. One type of "set", and one certain smell will *not* stop *all* critters. It takes a variety of sets as well as a variety of smells, tastes, and textures, and one must remember eye-appeal, to domesticate wild critters.

*Remember, take time to breathe! It boils down to the fact that each critter is an **Individual**.*

The individual is the FINAL judge. If the trap is "set" so the animal shows interest, it is *so* much easier to tame. However, if something is not quite to that individual's liking, it may not approach close enough to get caught.

As one with autism, it's often difficult to "get" humor, but little by little, we're learning to laugh at and with ourselves along this journey. So please accept this booklet with all its cheeky, sassy, bantering, facetious, playful intent.

Education and understanding of basic wildlife behaviors are the keys to success!

Autistic Critters Don't Seem to Like People

It's not that my neurodivergent wild thing doesn't like people—quite the opposite, really. It's just that, for him, being around folks is like being out in the hot sun. You can stand it for a while, maybe twenty minutes or so, but after that, it starts wearing on you: the noise, the lights, the constant buzz—it's often just too much at once.

Just like a trapper knows when to retreat to the shade after too long on the trail, your critter must find a way to step back when the world gets too loud. It's not about avoiding people—it's about knowing your limits.

That's why we equip him with the right tools and strategies to help him disengage before things get overwhelming. Sunglasses for the glare, earplugs for the noise, and a signal when he needs space—just like a trapper keeping his calm on the frontier.

So, when that twenty-minute mark comes up, it's not him turning his back on anyone. It's him protecting his peace and ensuring he can handle the next step with his mind and heart still intact.

Now, during those big holiday gatherings, when the house is full of laughter, chatter, and all the commotion that comes with family, you might see your wild thing slip off to a quiet corner with his phone. It's not avoidance, not by a long shot. It's his way of taking a breather, breaking all that social interaction into smaller, more manageable chunks. You see, for him, being in the thick of it is like walking through a forest. It's beautiful, but after a while, you've got to pause, catch your breath, and find your bearings.

That phone time in the corner? That's his tool for emotional management, a way to regulate his feelings and reset before heading back into the storm. Just like a trapper might sit by the fire after a long day in the wild, he's giving himself the space to recharge.

Breaking socializing into smaller blocks doesn't mean he's checked out-it means he's tuned in to his own limits, ensuring that when he's ready, he can rejoin the gathering without feeling overwhelmed. And that's a skill anyone could admire—knowing when to step back and return stronger.

The Challenge:
Interacting with people is often overwhelming.

Trapper's Solution:
You've got to arm your critter with mental tools that help him handle stress without snapping under pressure.

- **Try square breathing:** where he takes slow, deep, measured breaths in a steady rhythm, like pacing yourself on a long hike.

- **Or maybe meditation:** a way to center his thoughts when the world feels like it's closing in.

- **Music's another good one**—a simple pair of headphones can turn the loudest crowd into background noise, creating a little bubble of calm.

Each of these strategies is like giving him his own shield, something that keeps him from getting overwhelmed by it all.

These tools aren't just for bad moments—they'll help build a more Zen-like ability to manage chaos before it becomes too much. It's all about teaching awareness—how to recognize the onset of distress—and how to create that buffer, so instead of melting down, your wee beastie can handle the world with his own brand of quiet strength.

HER I took my son to the pool the other day. I thought it would be a perfect outing. However, the noise of the slapping water, the cacophony created by the boom box reverberating and echoing off the walls, and the chatter of the attendees in the water aerobics class quickly became too much.

He asked if he could just get out and use the hot tub for a bit. Of course, I said yes recognizing his need to isolate. He sat in the warm water for only a moment before he went to the most distant wall, sat on a bench, leaned back his head, closed his eyes, and just zoned out until the class was over.

I was very proud of him as he used his mind to create the quiet space he needed while waiting for his mom to get out of the pool.

Overwhelming Sensory Input Causes Pain

BE PREPARED!

Now, there's more to hiking through the wilderness than simply braving the weather and dodging predators. For an NT, a trip to the mall is a wonderful adventure, nothing to really worry about. However, when your wild thing is out and about, they learn quickly that loud noises and bright lights can feel like stepping straight into a bear trap—sharp, sudden, unexpected, intense. Too much of that sensory chaos, and it's like being all wrapped up, they struggle to breathe, trying to find a way out.

So, you've got to equip your wild one with the right tools—just like a woodsman would never go into the outback without their snares, lures, or flint. Sunglasses and earplugs are the survival gear built to help your beastie navigate the sensory wilderness without getting overwhelmed. They're not just accessories, they are vital.

These tools cut the noise, dim the glare, and give 'em the chance to walk through this world without springing every trap in the path. You wouldn't head into the woods unprepared, and neither should they. With the right gear, your wild thing can find its own way, safe and sound.

The Challenge:
Loud noises and bright lights may cause your critter actual physical pain.

Trapper's Solution:
Be Prepared. Outfit your wild thing with the right gear.

Help your beastie navigate the sensory wilderness without getting inundated.

Sunglasses not only protect sensitive eyes from intense visual stimulation but can also provide a perceived sense of protection, a barrier, between your wee beastie and the hostile world.

Earplugs or headphones provide several perks. They can be simple noise-canceling devices or a way to access pre-programmed personalized playlists.

Hoodies, what a strange item. But for the wild thing roaming the wilderness, it is often the perfect tool for having a "barrier" to the vastness of the universe.

There was a time when my boy wouldn't leave home without his hoodie. He told me he felt more protected with the hoodie wrapped around his head as he walked. Between that, his sunglasses and his scarf, he felt brave enough to walk home from school.

Loud noises and bright lights are only one type of sensory dissonance. Another type of extreme sensory disgust your critter may have experienced involves his taste buds. Is your critter extra picky and refuses to eat the food on their plate? Consistently, for years on end?

The friction this creates for the parent-child dynamic is stressful. Oh, that is stating it lightly! There is dissension, strife, or perhaps—all—out—war! This conflict occurs daily, multiple times a day. It's exhausting!

> **Food Challenge:**
> The taste, texture, and/or color of the food may be undesirable or disgusting. This means your critter may even have a gag reflex simply upon seeing the offending foodstuffs.
>
> **Trapper's Solution:**
> Be Creative. There are ways to help camouflage "undesirable" food.
> It's okay to play with your food!

Part of taming a beastie's palate is to learn what they will eat. One day my daughter put cooked pasta on her family's plates (one item she knows her critters enjoy). Then, instead of placing all the other ingredients on top like a Hawaiian Haystack, she placed them around the edge of the plate, more like a wreath. This day she gave them: peas, broccoli, carrot slices, hot dogs and olives. Everyone loved the carrots, hot dogs, and broccoli. About half of them chose peas. Nobody took the olives, which explained why other casseroles containing olives (such an offending food item!) were never consumed.

Another way to explore tastes and textures without anyone feeling threatened, or forced, is to make 3D models with your food before you eat. There were some days we would place a banana, kiwi slices, mango slices, pretzels, cheese squares (from block cheese), cheese circles (from string cheese), grapes, and strawberries on a plate. Then, we showed photos of cars: a Jalopy, a Model A, a limo, a sports car, and a truck. Then, the games began, and each person made their own car. On another day we made watercraft: motorboats, ships, yachts, canoes, rafts, sailboards, jet skis, barges, and more. The crazy creations our critters designed were epic.

We found while creating, they also ate a lot more. We had found a way to distract their focus from the food, and their dismay at being required to eat it. We were able to re-direct their energy into a creative pursuit where eating happened almost without thinking about it.

 One critter resisted eating any food except hot dogs. This was a struggle for more than a decade.

"Why don't you like the salad, Ben?"

"I like them well enough Mom, but they take so long to chew, it's so hard."

Eventually, greens became acceptable if they could be added to a variety of smoothies. Our critter created them so there was a different colored smoothie for each day. It was such a relief when, in a way that suited him, he learned to eat more healthily and began to participate in the process.

Be aware: sometimes it isn't about the food or how it tastes. If the texture or color is off it won't matter how it tastes. Some creatures simply can't take it.

Interestingly, we focus a lot on the 'pickiness' of our critters in the neurodivergent world because we deal with this idiosyncrasy (quirk, foible, trait, eccentricity, oddity) every day, every meal. However, one needs to consider the fact that there are foods out there they may never care for. One very important thing to watch out for, or be aware of, is an allergic reaction as opposed to simple orneriness.

Let's consider cilantro. We discovered the reason James doesn't like to eat it, and it isn't because he's 'picky.' As a genealogist I became interested in the genetic diversity of our family. With the help of a DNA test, not only did we discover some wonderful things about our family tree, but we also discovered some pre-disposition to certain likes and dislikes, all scientifically found in our DNA. Did you know up to 14% of the population has the same reaction to cilantro as James? He is one of those that doesn't find a refreshing, citrusy taste when he bites into this herb. To him, this herb tastes like soap. No wonder he is vigilant about making certain it doesn't *ever* get put into his food. Can you blame him? Not me. James has long fought the battle with others saying he is too picky. He has learned to just look at them and say, "I'm not picky, I'm discerning..."

On a similar note, when I was a young girl, eating our vegetables at the dinner table was important. My sister never wanted to eat tomatoes and religiously took them out of any dish found on her plate. This, of course, was not acceptable to our parents. Yes, there were disagreements over this issue.

During harvest season as we were cleaning up the garden, there were quite a few late tomatoes still on the vine. As children do, we began to have a tomato war. It was so much fun, but didn't last long. My sister began to have a severe reaction to the tomatoes on her skin, and soon there were blisters. We learned she was allergic to certain proteins in raw fruits and veggies. Interesting note, she can eat them cooked. These proteins are broken down (denatured) during cooking, which makes them less likely to cause harm. Our poor mother felt so bad about the tomatoes she had required her to eat prior to this discovery. I remember her sorrow over it and saying how much pain must have been endured because she simply didn't know it was blistering the skin on the inside. Mama cried.

> **To parents and caregivers:**
> *Allow yourself grace for what you didn't know.*
> *We're all doing the best we can.*

There was a day my grandmother came to visit, and we began to help her prepare a wonderful dinner. I was tasked with peeling the potatoes. I was a little whiney about the heat and the chore, pretty much the worst parts of an "I don't wanna" varmint. In fact, I'll bet I was horribly obnoxious as my discomfort grew. I told them my eyes were itchy, and my skin was unhappy. After a while grandmother took a good look at me, took me to the kitchen sink and began to wash all traces of the potato off my skin. My eyes were swollen and red, and my face was a little puffy too. That was the day we learned that raw potatoes and I were not friends.

On another day, I was walking through the garden with my dad surveying some of the crops. He unearthed a potato, washed it off, and said, "Here, Diana, have a bite. These are delicious raw." I wasn't sure about that, but bit into the potato, began to chew and swallowed. I didn't like it. Within just a few minutes my mouth was itchy, I got a rash, and I began to have trouble breathing. To this day I avoid raw potatoes.

Among all the fun things we teach our children from colors to music to numbers, we may want to add a list of descriptive words above and beyond emotions and emojis. They need to let us know what texture works for them, and what doesn't. Have you thought about any of these texture words recently?

Buttery	Greasy	Runny
Boiled	Gritty	Smooth
Chewy	Hard	Soft
Chopped	Juicy/wet	Spongy
Creamy	Lumpy	Sticky
Crispy	Melted	Tender
Crumbly	Moist	Tough
Crunchy	Oily	Thick
Gooey	Roasted	
Grated	Rough	

Another fun list is food flavors: Sweet, salty, sour, bitter, savory, tart, spicy, and smoky.

Changes In Routine Are Distressing

Unexpected changes can be like sudden storms rolling in over the horizon, that may catch your wild thing off guard, throwing him off course. You can see that thunderhead building on the horizon, dark and foreboding, ready to unleash a downpour at any moment. One minute, the sun is shining and the next, his internal winds are howling, leaving him scrambling out of control, and unable to regain his footing. That's why it's crucial to have a backup plan in place, just in case. This gives you a safety net to mitigate the approaching, possible meltdown.

The Challenge:
Unexpected changes are disruptive to your critter's pre-programmed day.

Trapper's First Solution:
It's in your best interest to help your beastie know the lay of the land, to know what the schedule is for the day, so they are not caught unawares. Sometimes this might include reminders for several days in advance.

Trapper's Second Solution:
Always have a backup plan.

AROMA: If the plans simply must shift, have a familiar item or aroma (often an essential oil) on hand to bring comfort on a different sensory pathway.

My granddaughter, Mir, gets overly emotional even a day in advance as we endeavor to let her know there are changes afoot. Recently the plan was to attend a LEGO building day at the local library. Then, her mother came down seriously ill and we knew the children would need to remain at home while their mom recuperated. As I was relating some of the changes, she began to wail. We're talking ear-splitting "But I wanted to go build LEGO's", accompanied by intense sobbing, shallow breathing, and was well on her way to hyperventilation. She went from calm to hurricane in less than a moment. We called her name. Nothing. I tried, "Mir, that's enough!" Nothing. We tried holding her. We tried wrapping her in my big overcoat, next to me. Nope. "Mir! There's no need to cry. Listen up, hon, I want to tell you something."

Sobbing continued with, "But I can't stop crying! It won't stop..." and more tears.

We added essential oils, one of her favorite scents, right under her nose and coaxed her to breathe deeply, still safely wrapped in my coat and my arms. It took some time, but this had a remarkable effect. She began to breathe more normally. Thank goodness. She had melted down before we even had a chance to inform the group of sisters that we had a backup plan for them. Uncle Ben has boxes of LEGOs, and he was going to bring them over so they could create with them all day long, not just for one hour at the library. This helped keep her calm once we had reached equilibrium again. Whew! Crisis averted.

TOUCH: a familiar handshake or a finger game can be a useful diversion. Keep a "go-to bag" on hand and prepacked with items to entertain when the unexpected happens. We have items that can only be played with while traveling. We have some that can only be accessed at bedtime. A compression vest or shirt can add an extra layer of comfort. It is like having a warm hug without being forced to deal with or encounter a person.

Magnetic pictures are tactile. The ability to manipulate the pieces physically, as well as using the imagination to tell a story, often brings satisfaction to creative play.

TASTE/TEXTURE: sometimes distraction is helpful, and a small snack might be the answer. Perhaps your furbaby is a little "hangry"?

TO-GO FOOD. Crunchy veggies or fruit wedges with dip can be a good place to begin. Carrots, cucumbers, olives, pickles, celery, cheese sticks, pretzels, and the list goes on and on. Be creative. Our little ones appreciate their travel food in individual ziplock baggies. This helps them maintain "control" of their meal. My late-diagnosed wild thing loves French burnt peanuts while traveling. Be aware this can change without a moment's notice. The red dye has become a digestive issue that bothers him, so now he goes for the Sahale Snack® Banana Rum Pecans instead.

I recently heard about another kind of chewable. There are adorable necklaces in many styles developed as sensory jewelry for children with a need for something more after they've outgrown the typical binkie/pacifier. What a unique idea that has great potential for soothing and reducing distress.

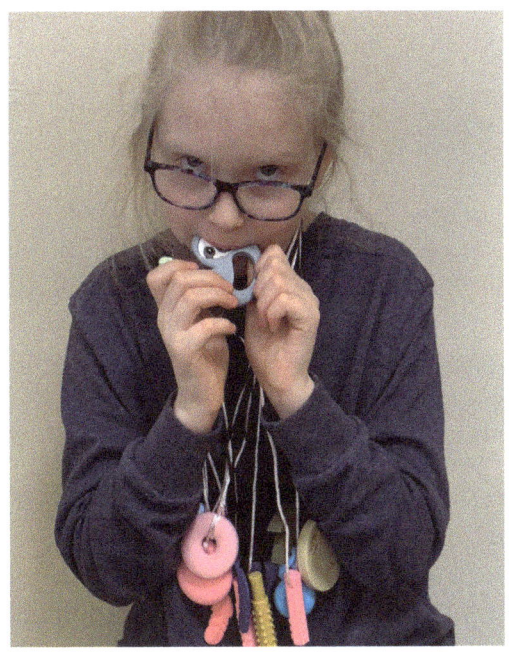

HER When a varmint melts down, it is not a personal attack. It's best to sigh and take a deep breath. The "attack" may feel personal, especially when someone focuses their verbal, emotional, and sometimes physical frustration on you. But your tiny critter feels trapped, out of control, and needs to adjust. Your furbaby has become like a wounded badger. It is never a good idea to corner them.

HIM Conversely, there have been times when I didn't "vent" but internalized, becoming quiet, reflective, and withdrawn. This resulted in others thinking I was mad when I was not. I needed time to process and organize my thoughts in an attempt to calm myself, eliminate stress, and eventually feel like talking. Trying to communicate through the haze of confusion that always attends volatile emotions is nearly impossible. I know, as a neurodivergent, it is that way for me every time. We don't "*grow out of it.*" Hopefully, over time, we learn to manage our distress better.

HER It's okay to say "no" to sudden invitations, even good ones like visiting cousins. If your critter is excited for the current day's activities, it's okay to turn down what we would perceive as a positive addition. Even though it's good and would most likely be enjoyed, it also could be "too much." Know your critter!

We Struggle with Social Cues

Just like a seasoned trapper learns to read the 'lay of the land' by recognizing tracks and signs, it's essential to teach our wee wild things how to 'read the room.' The subtle cues, the shifts in energy, the tension in voices, the way people move, can all tell a story about what's happening around him.

By paying attention to these signals, he can gauge when the atmosphere is friendly or when it might be turning chaotic, allowing him to respond appropriately, or to exit. It's about helping him develop the instincts to sense when to engage and when to step back, just as a trapper knows when to approach a potential catch or when to wait patiently in the shadows.

> **The Social Challenge:**
> For the beloved ND furbaby, reading social cues is nearly impossible. It is elusive and confusing—and may feel like trying to track a fox in the snow...blind-folded.

Ninety-three percent of communication is "non-verbal." While 7% is verbal, 38% is vocal (tone, pitch, pace, volume, inflection) and 55% is visual (facial expression, body language, gestures, humor).

Many of our famed spectrum dwellers are completely oblivious to 93% of the clues around them in standard communication. Thus, they are flying blind.

Interestingly, since they often don't recognize this, they don't realize they're missing "critical, need-to-know information." Consequently, they may reach incorrect conclusions based on the slimmest margins while trying to read the environment around them.

> **Trapper's Solution:**
> There are apps to help with learning social cues.
>
> Additionally, visual supports, such as AAC, help many with verbal issues express their ideas by using images. What a gift this tool is!

Some available tools may include role-playing, practicing social interactions and cues from different scenarios. You may use stories to help explain a social cue or an appropriate response. This may help provide structure, breaking down abstract concepts into concrete actions.

Observation and mimicry. Encourage your critter to observe social interactions or conversations and mimic appropriate responses.

This hits a nerve for me. There are so many nuances in each interaction. Learning specific cues and responses is like saying that all situations have an appropriate response—this has not been true for me. Learning and properly navigating the intricacies of the give-and-take social dance called communication has been so difficult. Even after sixty-four years, there is _so_ much that escapes me.

"Practicing social cues" is what the school system taught us in the late 2000's. Patience and doing them over and over is the key. We were counseled to provide opportunities to rehearse these skills so they can be used in real-life settings.

At this time (2024), this skill set still eludes our younger wee beasties. In fact, it still eludes my late-diagnosed critter, too. He tells me the best life skill in this area of confusing social cues is to remain silent until the social terrain comes back into focus. That way, he doesn't embarrass himself. That is his current coping mechanism. This has been our experience, yours may be different.

Through positive reinforcement, and celebrating every small success, you can help your furbaby develop amazing self-confidence.

We May Lack Focus

Concentrating on tasks can be as tricky as setting a snare in just the right spot. A trapper knows that even a slight miscalculation can mean the difference between success and failure; similarly, finding the focus to tackle a task requires precision and mindfulness.

Distractions lurk around every corner, ready to pull attention away just as a curious animal might wander off, avoiding the trap. It's about understanding what works best for our wild things. Creating an environment free from distractions, breaking tasks into smaller steps, and using timers as reminders may help us keep on track.

Challenge:
Concentrating on tasks can feel so futile!

Trapper's Solution:
Create a distraction-free environment during chores, events, or tasks, akin to a trapper's quiet hideaway. Provide needed structure to clearly see the end goal.

Using visual supports like timetables, checklists, and social stories is like having a well-marked trail through the wilderness. Just as a trapper relies on maps and signs to navigate the landscape, these tools can help our critters break tasks down into smaller, more easily attainable goals.

Timetables provide a clear layout of what to expect throughout the day, while checklists offer a step-by-step guide, making daunting tasks feel manageable. Social stories can prepare him for new situations, illustrating what to anticipate and how to respond, much like a trapper scouting the area before setting up camp.

Unplug: Turn off the TV and radio, and minimize all other distractions. Common issues your furbaby may encounter are many and varied. It's not just about our electronics, though. Here are some you may not have considered.

Wildlife Sounds: Animal calls, the rustling of leaves, or sudden movements. These can divert attention and disturb your critter's focus, from inside the home, and out.

Weather Changes: Wind suddenly rattling the windows, or rain or snow can disrupt concentration, making it challenging to stay focused on the current task.

Fellow Wild Things: The actions of nearby beasties can be distracting, whether through noise, movement, or conversation. Heck, even hearing another's breathing can be enough to complicate your critter's day.

Personal Thoughts: Worries and other things on their mind often take focus away from current tasks, making it difficult to remain present, in the moment.

Equipment Issues: Problems with gear, empty water bottles, broken pencils, ripped paper, itchy tags in clothes. The same as missing equipment, a broken trap, or a tangled fishing line can shift focus and require immediate attention.

Scent and Smoke: Strong smells from cooking, campfires, or other nearby activities can distract from the natural scents of the environment that are crucial for self-awareness and focus.

Changes in Light: Shifting light, whether from the sun setting or clouds moving in, impacts concentration.

Sounds: You've created a perfect quiet room complete with a miniature waterfall and terrarium. However, the sounds of flowing water have become distracting. Feel free to re-evaluate and re-do your sanctuary.

Take movement breaks: Our critters have behaved SO much better when allowed free, unrestrained, blood-pumping activities in between brain work.

Feeling drowsy or sluggish: Sometimes a healthy snack gives your critter more energy and helps your mind stay sharp.

Use deep breathing exercises. This skill can help your critter calm down and reduce stress levels.

Picking activities your furbaby (or wild thing) is interested in has an enormous impact on attention span.

All the things listed above are huge distractions. We've discussed tools to help our critters stay focused, and on task. Sometimes our wee ones don't need another reminder to "focus!" Sometimes, they need a new tactile experience and the room to "play" as they do their work.

Try this on for size. When practicing writing, we've discovered through both research and experience that it is often a difficult, difficult thing for them to get their ideas from their brains onto the paper. These little ones endure enormous amounts of frustration, and it often harms their self-esteem. It's time to give them a break! I decided to really "change it up" one day. Instead of the traditional paper and pencil at a desk, I took my beasties into the kitchen where jelly-roll pans filled with pudding were waiting for them. Oh yes, we practiced our penmanship that day, in pudding. "Mom, Mom! I think this is the best "A" on this row, what do you think?!" and "Mom, what will grandma say when I tell her I ate my homework?!" These are some of the best memories.

We Seek Comfort, Order, and Creativity

For our ND critters, having familiar and soothing items is essential to creating that sense of comfort, much like a trapper relies on a cozy campfire and a trusty cot after a long day in the wilderness.

Just as a trapper gathers wood for a fire to ward off the chill of the night, our critters need those comforting items to help them feel grounded and at ease.

Challenge:

Feeling comfortable can be as rare as spotting a white stag in the wild—an elusive moment that brings a sense of awe, peace, safety, and tranquility.

Trapper's Solution:

Surround your neurodivergent critter with familiar and soothing items; a favorite blanket, a calming sensory toy, a service animal, or a cherished book. This helps provide that warm, familiar feeling, wrapping them in a sense of security amidst the chaos found in the world.

What does your critter like best? What would create their favorite "den," "space," or "corner?" Let's get creative!

This Trapper's Thoughts: Our wild furbabies have been interested in holes. In the wild, these holes can be up a tree, in a log lying on the ground, in a stump, at the base of a tree or boulder, or under a flat rock. These holes can be small, tight, and snug. Like the size of a mouse, or simply cozy and about the size a bear would use for a den, with a little wiggle room.

Some creative spaces that are cozy for children could include hanging chairs or a sensory swing. Body socks are unique for play and designed with sensory issues in mind. Pillows and stuffed toys with soft textures, combined with weighted blankets, are always welcome.

Your creative critter space doesn't need to be fancy. Many of our favorite "hide-aways" have been as simple as a blanket thrown across the kitchen table that reached to the floor. This created the perfect "bear den" for imaginative play. Throw in a pillow and a few toys or books, and you have a thoroughly thrilled urchin. Quiet, creative spaces provide the comfort and familiarity needed to relax and recharge.

Most of our wee beasties have complained long and loud about the itchy tags inside their clothing. We have long since cut out any remaining spare cloth that caused issues. Comfortable clothing is paramount to happy play, happy rest time, and a happy life.

Part of our consistent bedtime routine involves a preferred music playlist or even a white noise machine. Whether the sounds be familiar ones like that of ocean waves or chirping birds in the background, each critter has its preferred habitat.

Some of your critters may be afraid of the dark. Many years ago, one of ours chose to have a lava lamp in her room. It brought her joy as she nodded off to sleep.

Praise your varmint when they complete a project or reach a milestone, no matter how small. Drop by drop we can fill up our precious critter's emotional pitcher. We talk about the things that bring our ND family comfort with soft spaces, blankets, and swings, colors, and environmental mood yet we must remember verbal comfort and inspiration too.

There's nothing like praise to bring comfort to our psyche. There's nothing quite like that feeling when you're wrapped in a sweet blanket of affirmation and acceptance. This helps provide a precious space of emotional peace. With these tools, our "deer" ones may have the courage to face the future and have sufficient hope to buoy their spirits when the going gets rough.

| Praise | Support |
| Encourage | Love |

Synopsis

PEOPLE ISSUES

Focus on proactive strategies like square breathing (inhale to the count of four, hold it for four, release for the count of four, pause for the count of four, repeat), meditation, and music to help your "critter" build a calm, controlled response to overwhelming situations. Here are some suggestions:

- Headphones
- Fidget toys
- Phone time in the corner of a room during holiday gatherings
- Break social interaction into smaller blocks of time or have a trusty escape plan to return to his ordered "creative space"

SENSORY ISSUES

In a world filled with an abundance of sensory stimuli, finding balance can be a challenge. By fostering a greater understanding of sensory needs, we can help our "wee beasties" create their own personalized strategies for emotional regulation. You might try the following:

- Sunglasses
- Earplugs, noise cancellers
- Personalized, soothing playlist
- Dimmable light or lava lamp
- Blue-light blocking glasses (computers)
- UV blocking glasses (sunlight)
- Body sock
- Bubble tube or water feature

Food – All the vitamins and minerals available in delicious cuisine are lost to our critters if they won't eat any of it. Much of the taste, texture, and nuances of flavor simply don't exist for them. Here are just a few ideas.

Camouflage for nutrition – possibilities:

- Shred carrots or zucchini into the spaghetti sauce: this *may* result in getting a serving of veggies into an extremely picky eater
- Crush a vitamin pill in ¼ cup of applesauce
- Add mashed cauliflower into mashed potatoes
- One drop of doTERRA® OnGuard® essential oil in your oatmeal (ratio: 4 C cooked oatmeal to 1 drop OnGuard®).
- Use a blender to puree veggies into your dips, or soups, e.g. carrots, zucchini, or spinach. Try them. They have a reduced imprint when being added to other foods and lack a strong aroma—making them perfect for achieving the mission objective.

After timed creative play to create your "food model", set a timer for devouring it. This often brings laughter, joy, and silliness.

- **Needed:** toothpicks, or peanut butter for glue
- **Fruit options:** Grapes, apples, strawberries, blueberries, bananas, kiwifruit, mango, etc.

- **Veggie options:** carrot rounds, peas, spinach leaves, broccoli, cucumbers, cauliflower, fries (potato or sweet potato), 'tater tots, corn, kale leaves, etc.
- **Milk options:** string cheese, various kinds of cheese cut into a variety of shapes.
  - As kids are playing, if they won't touch it, they probably won't eat it either.

If you have a slightly older critter, take them shopping with you and let them choose what looks appealing. Of course, always ask them if they're relatively sure they can get it down, uhm-swallow it, later.

ROUTINE DISRUPTION

Be ready for a meltdown if none of your backup plans prove useful. Also, and this is huge, don't take it personally. It isn't. Breathe deeply. Access your well of patience. Release your Breath. You've got this.

- Just as a trapper learns to read the skies and prepare for the elements, your wild thing needs these tools to navigate the unpredictability of life. A solid backup plan helps us all weather the storm, hopefully avoiding the deluge and maintaining our equilibrium.

- First, as an NT, do your best to help your beastie know what's on the schedule, sometimes days in advance, so they're not caught unaware. This is the best medicine!

- **AROMA:** If the plans simply must shift, have a familiar item or aroma (often an essential oil) on hand to bring comfort on a different sensory pathway.
    - Roller bottle filled with favorite essential oil

- **TOUCH:** a familiar handshake or a finger game can be a useful diversion. Keep a "to-go bag" on hand and pre-packed to entertain when the unexpected happens. We have items that are only played with while traveling.
    - Compression vest or shirt
    - Cooling towel
    - Magnetic pictures
    - Weighted blanket
    - Fidget spinner

SOCIAL CUES, DID I MISS SOMETHING?

This skill fosters a greater understanding of social dynamics. It empowers our often-clueless critters to navigate social situations confidently, ensuring they feel more in control when the landscape changes unexpectedly.

- Teach them to pause in the doorway and take a moment to observe the room and who's talking.
- Role play. Practice social interactions and cues from different scenarios
- For the non-verbal, investigate PECS or AAC tools, or apps to assist with visual cues

TO FOCUS OR NOT TO FOCUS

With the right approach, we can hone focus and 'set a snare for success', catching those moments of concentration before they slip away into the wilderness of distraction.

- By incorporating visual supports, we help our wee beasties find their way through the maze of life's responsibilities, ensuring that each step taken is one closer to success, without feeling overwhelmed by the journey ahead.
- Pudding Activity

COMFORT IS REQUIRED

By surrounding our fur babies with what they know and love, they can navigate their environment with more confidence, transforming even the most overwhelming situation into a place where they can thrive and find peace.

- Weighted blankets
- Soft textures
- Hanging chairs
- Sensory swings
- White noise machine
- Quiet spaces
- Familiar music playlist
- Positive verbal encouragement

Historical References

WHAT IS A TRAPPER?

A trapper is a hunter who uses traps and snares to catch animals in their natural habitat. The trapper's knowledge of specific animal habits and movements helps him strategically place a snare for maximum efficiency and the desired outcome.

Synonyms: deerstalker, falconer, fisherman, howker, huntress, huntsman, and woodsman.

WHAT WOULD A TRAPPER WEAR?

Trappers in the 1800s wore simple undershirts of flannel or cotton. It was necessary to wear multiple layers of clothing to stay warm in the winter. When those wore out, they made shirts with animal skins. Their outer garments were made of buckskin with seams ending in fringed leather. The fringes were used as string or thread to repair clothing, moccasins, and equipment. Buckskin is traditionally made

from the tanned hide of a deer, sheep, goat, moose, buffalo, elk, antelope, or cow. This type of clothing was readily available through trade with the Indians.

Like people today, trappers had several styles and choices for comfortable wear. Some preferred to wear more manufactured goods, like cloth pants and shirts. Others adopted the clothing worn by the Native Americans among whom they lived, which meant being clothed head to toe in buckskins.

Have you ever heard of a "brogan"? This was a solid, stout leather shoe that many trappers wore. It was too short to be called a boot and came further up the foot than a simple shoe, reaching to the ankle. The slang for this was 'work shoe' or 'clodhopper.'

- **Hats:** Made from wool or leather.
- **Belts:** Made from leather and used to hold other tools, like knives or pistols.

- **Moccasins:** Made from leather. They were worn tall, or shorter, depending on weather and environmental conditions.

- **Leggings:** Made from supple buckskin and worn instead of trousers.

- **Breechcloth:** A long, wide piece of cloth hung from a leather belt, designed to cover the loins.

TOOLS OF THE TRAPPER'S TRADE

What could be found in a "possibles bag"? And why is it called that?

Traditionally, this bag carried various small items that a trapper might "possibly" use during the day. Basic tools like a knife, a powder measure, ammunition (like lead balls and patches), flint and steel for starting fires, or an awl, are often included. They may have carried some basic first-aid supplies, being well-versed in certain common herbs easily found in the wild. Mullein's soft, wide leaves were sometimes used as an extra layer of padding in shoes to help prevent blisters.

If you had a "Possibles Bag" for your little critter, what would it include? What do you need most?

What do you need just a little later? Are you prepared for the inescapable? Because that meltdown, that sense of overwhelm, that loss of immediate emotional self-control is coming. It is inevitable.

HER One day I got a call at work and was asked to get to the middle school as quickly as possible. Ben had had a meltdown and was currently being kept in a small meeting room, severely agitated and pacing, waiting for his mother to arrive.

What happened? Well, there was a difference of opinion between Ben and the principal. While making his rounds behind the school during recess, he saw several boys playing with some large sticks. He told the boys they needed to put the sticks down, for safety's sake. Most obeyed, but Ben was annoyed. He was enjoying the game and didn't appreciate this disruption. The principal later told me Ben put down the stick, but followed him around, growling his discontent for a while. Eventually, Ben wandered off.

The bells rang signaling the end of recess. The principal tried to get back inside with some of the other students from the playground but couldn't get in. Ben stood there inside the school, watching. They never told me very many details about this part of the day, but I believe Ben may have been really pleased with himself for having locked the principal out of the school.

As soon as I arrived the staff brought me quickly to the small room. Ben was pacing up and down, raising his arms into the air, and voicing his discontent. I watched for only a moment and quickly checked my purse, finding the roller bottle filled with doTERRA®'s essential oils of Wild Orange and Douglas Fir, properly diluted and ready to use. This was my "possibles bag go-to" for Ben's desperate situations. I sat him in an office chair, sat across from him knee-to-knee, pulled out my essential oils, and began to give him an Aroma Touch hand massage. He calmed down very quickly, and then we were able to talk. Sometimes a good aroma, some gentle hand massaging, and a calm voice can work miracles.

Your "possibles" bag will have different things in it, depending on the age of the child you are prepared for. Regardless of any variables in age, there are some simple rules that are important to observe when deciding on the contents of your "possibles" bag.

- **Keep it simple** – You are not trying to build a second home in your pack. Packing too much is simply too heavy. Pack simple, reliable things to cover your critter's basic needs.

- **Be self-sufficient** – Pack what you need that can be used both individually and together, to save space. If you pack an item that needs something else [which you don't already have with you], forget it. In the middle of chaos, the chances of finding it would be slim to none.

- **Only pack what you need** – remember the goal is to survive, together. If you don't need it to survive, leave it behind.

- **Change it up!** – if your critter can handle variety, it does add some spice to life. Mine could always wonder, "What did grandma put in here this time...?"

To be defined as a "possibles" bag, you'll need to decide what it will look like, and how it will function. Do you want it to be a neck pouch, an over-the-shoulder bag, or a backpack? What size suits your current needs?

Some of our critters are a little OCD about the cleanliness of their hands. For them, a little sanitizer and hand moisturizer are important. Others appreciate a good ChapStick® for their lips (which are chronically dry). Mostly, the contents have been about keeping little hands occupied and minds busy: four Crayola®, a small coloring book, a story tin filled with Noah's Ark magnets, a fidget spinner, a favorite small stuffed animal, pre-packaged snacks (crackers, peanuts, veggie baggie), essential oil roller bottles filled with their favorite scents, a small matchbox car or airplane, etc. Some of our critters are growing up. While traveling, they appreciate a good app on their phone, allowing them to keep up with their favorite music station, game, audible book or blog.

POSSIBLES POUCH POSSIBILITIES

Here are some excellent items to include in a "possibles" bag designed to help prevent and manage overwhelm or meltdowns for autistic children and adults.

POSSIBLES BAG CHECKLIST
3 – 7 YEARS

Comfort Items

- Favorite stuffed animal or small blanket
- Comfort objects (weighted lap pad, pacifier, lovey, etc.)
- Photo of family or a favorite place

Sensory Tools

- Noise-canceling headphones or ear defenders to block overwhelming sounds
- Fidget toys (e.g., soft squishy toys, spinners, pop-its) to help regulate sensory input
- Chewable sensory toys (necklaces, bracelets, ring pop)
- Sunglasses or hat to reduce light sensitivity

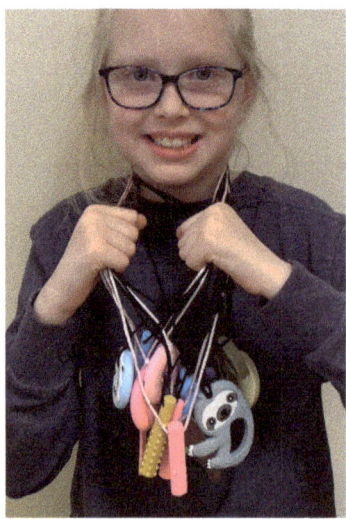

Distraction Tools

- Small picture book or board book
- Coloring book with crayons
- Small bubbles or pinwheel
- Interactive toy (light-up toys, push-button sound toys, etc.)
- Tablet or smartphone loaded with calming apps, simple games, music or favorite videos

Snacks and Drinks

- Non-messy snacks (fruit snacks, crackers, Cheerios, etc.)
- Sippy cup or spill-proof water bottle

Emergency and Communication Tools

- Picture communication cards or a portable AAC device
- Emergency contact card (with child's info)
- Comfort strategy reminders (for caregivers)

Practical Items

- Wipes and travel-size sanitizer
- Change of clothes (shirt, pants, underwear)
- Portable cooling towel or fan for temperature regulation

Calming Scents (if tolerated)

- Roll-on essential oils
- Scented item with a familiar and comforting smell

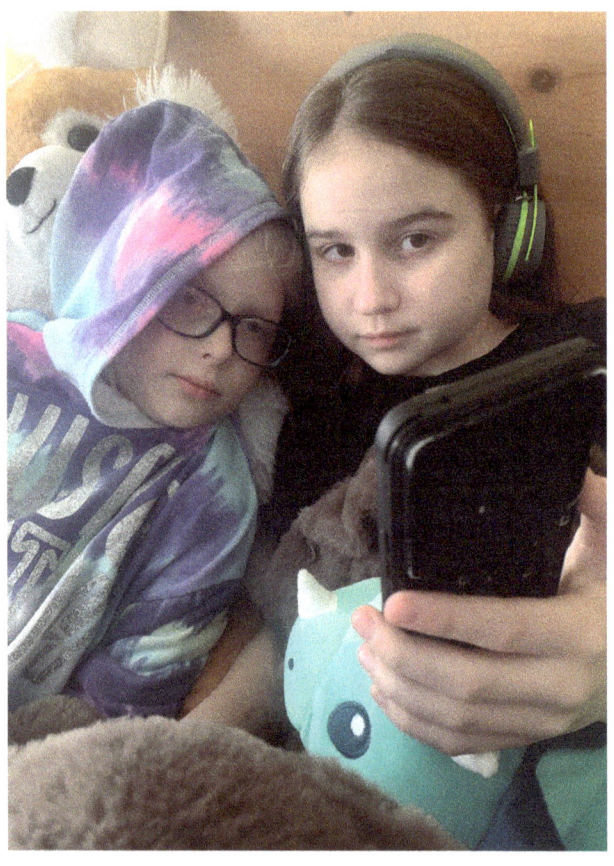

POSSIBLES BAG CHECKLIST
8 – 12 YEARS

Sensory Tools
- Noise-canceling headphones or earplugs
- Fidget toys (e.g., stress balls, spinners, pop-its, tangle, etc.)
- Chewable necklace or sensory item
- Weighted lap pad or small weighted item for comfort and grounding
- Sunglasses or hat to reduce light sensitivity

Comfort Items
- Favorite stuffed animal or small plushie
- Comfort object (pacifier, lovey, etc.)
- Comfort photo of family, a favorite place or sentimental item
- Soft travel-size blanket or scarf

Distraction Tools
- Picture book, puzzle book, or graphic novel
- Notebook and pens/pencils
- Small toy or figurines
- Tablet or smartphone loaded with calming apps, basic games, music + headphones

Snacks and Drinks

- Non-messy snacks (fruit snacks, granola bar, crackers, etc.)
- Water bottle or favorite drink (spill-proof lid)

Emergency and Communication Tools

- Picture communication cards, a notebook, or a portable AAC device
- Emergency contact card or bracelet (with child's info)
- Comfort strategy reminders (for caregivers)
- Calming strategy checklist

Practical Items

- Wipes and travel-size sanitizer
- Change of clothes (shirt, pants, underwear)
- Portable cooling towel or fan for temperature regulation

Calming Scents (if tolerated)

- Roll-on essential oils (such as doTERRA® Serenity) for easing anxiety
- Scented item with a familiar and comforting smell.

POSSIBLES BAG CHECKLIST
13 – 17 YEARS

Sensory Tools

- Over-ear noise-canceling headphones or discreet earplugs
- Small portable fidget toys (e.g., stress balls, fidget cubes, spinners, pop-its, etc.)
- Chewable necklace or inconspicuous sensory item
- Weighted lap pad or small weighted item for comfort and grounding.
- Clip-on/tinted sunglasses to reduce light sensitivity

Comfort Items

- Small item with sentimental value (keychain, photo, etc.)
- Hoodie or scarf with a calming texture
- Access to a stress-relief app on their phone or device

Distraction Tools

- Picture book, manga, or graphic novel
- Notebook and pens for doodling or journaling
- Favorite Tablet or smartphone loaded with calming apps, music or favorite videos, intermediate or advanced games
- Portable puzzle game (e.g., Rubik's Cube)

Snacks and Drinks

- Healthy snacks (dried fruit, granola bar, trail mix, etc.)
- Water bottle or travel cup with a secure lid

Emergency and Communication Tools

- Discreet communication cards or notes on their phone
- Emergency contact card or medical ID bracelet (with child's info)
- Quick reference guide with personal calming strategies

Practical Items
- Wipes and travel-size sanitizer
- Lip balm
- Change of clothes (shirt, pants, underwear)
- Portable cooling towel or fan for temperature regulation

Calming Scents (if tolerated)
- Roll-on essential oils (teen-friendly scents like citrus, outdoor pine, and peppermint)
- Scented item with a familiar and comforting smell

Hopefully, this gives you a solid starting point for packing your own 'possibles' bag. Remember, there is no medical or psychological evidence that any certain age is too old for comfort objects. Basically, if the *wild thing still needs it, it is too soon to give it up*.

We hope you and your little critter (or late-diagnosed person) continue to navigate life's wild terrain safely, with a sense of preparedness and adventure.

LATE DIAGNOSED
(anything after age twenty-one)

 I use a 'possibles' bag too. I have one for driving and one for survival in a crowd. They are a little different and may contain some of the following elements:

- **Music.** Music is calming, if we're near a lot of people, music covers the chaos of the crowd. Earphones cause pressure irritation after a while when they are in the ear. I prefer the ones that are "out of the ear," known as "bone conduction headphones."

- **Audio books** – may help you pass the time as you drive. I like music better.

- **Munchies.** I'm a creature of motion; I rarely sit still. I don't like enforced immobility. A good conversation with my wife helps on a long drive, too. But if that's not available, munchies give a sense of something to do besides being stuck going in a monotonous straight line. If there is a curvy road, I don't need munchies because the road requires my fully focused attention. I love driving. But when there is a long, long straight road, I reach for a different sensory activity. I like beef jerky, carrot sticks, a trail mix, or a lightly sweet chewy food.

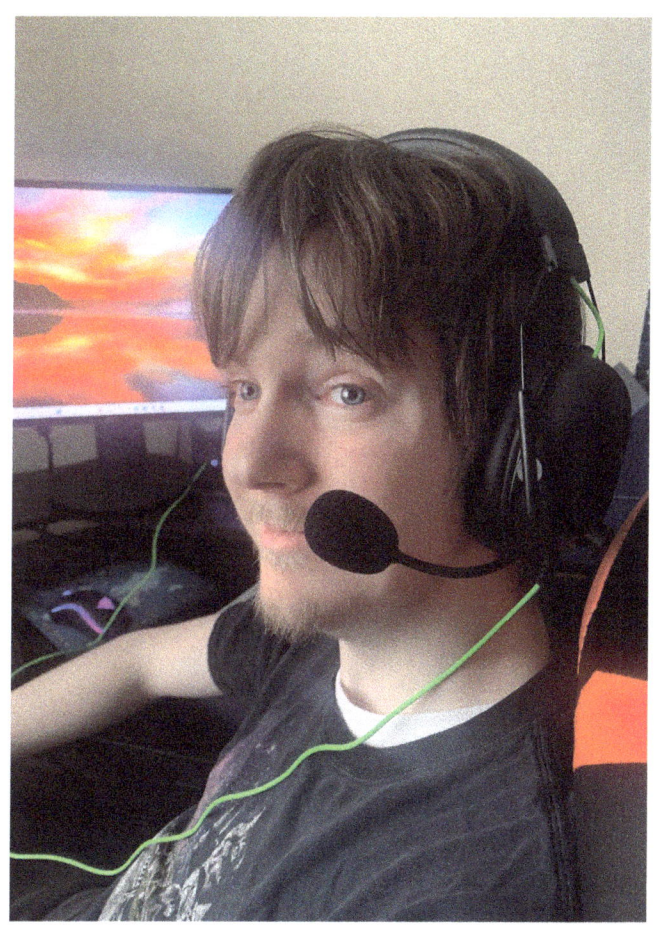

VOCABULARY
...and a linguistics lesson...

AAC = "Augmentative and Alternative Communication" device, a tool that helps people with speech or communication difficulties to "talk" when they cannot speak naturally.

ND = Neurodivergent, on the spectrum

NT = Neurotypical, not on the spectrum

Neurodivergent is the opposite of neurotypical.

Neurodivergent refers to an individual. You are neurodivergent if you have been diagnosed with a developmental or learning disorder, such as autism, dyslexia, ADHD, or Tourette's syndrome.

We need to embrace using the term "neurodivergent" when describing "you're different from me, a neurotypical person."

On a purely linguistic level, referring to someone as neurodiverse is incorrect.

Strictly speaking, neurodiverse refers to the entire human race. It's a word with a broad meaning and describes the concept that "we are different from one another." *Diversity* is a term belonging to groups, not a person.

Michael Sorensen   Preston Sorensen

Want to attend a **Rendezvous** (an enactment of Mountain Man Meetings from 1821–1840)? There are many Rendezvous events. Axe throwing, archery, and marksmanship contests are held along with vendor booths filled with interesting projects and historical information. Feel free to find your inner Mountain Man!

ABOUT THE AUTHOR

Diana is the proud mother of nine children. With a lifetime of experience navigating the many paths of parenthood, she has learned to appreciate the unique strengths each child brings to the world. Alongside her neurodivergent spouse, she finds humor in the everyday moments that make their life together an adventure.

Her love for gardening grounds her in nature, where she finds peace and inspiration.

In her spare time, she cherishes moments with her grandchildren and dedicates herself to helping others explore their family histories, combining research with field trips that bring stories of the past to life.

With special affection for the children and grandchildren who taught us so much over the past several decades. Watching you grow, learn, and develop into your best selves has been a joy.

We're so proud of you all!

Dad and Mom
"Papa" and "Mimi"

www.ingramcontent.com/pod-product-compliance
Lightning Source LLC
Chambersburg PA
CBHW052131030426
42337CB00028B/5108